MANUAL OF INSTRUC...

Edinburgh Reading Test 1

(Forms A & B)

MANUAL
THIRD EDITION

Educational Assessment Unit,
University of Edinburgh

HODDER
EDUCATION
AN HACHETTE UK COMPANY

Orders: please contact Bookpoint Ltd, 130 Milton Park, Abingdon, Oxon OX14 4SB.
Telephone: (44) 01235 827720, Fax: (44) 01235 400454. Lines are open from 9.00 to 5.00,
Monday to Saturday, with a 24-hour message answering service.
You can also order through our website: www.hoddereducation.co.uk

British Library Cataloguing in Publication Data
A catalogue record for this title is available from The British Library

ISBN-13: 978 0 340 80119 2

Impression number   10
Year   2013

Printed in Great Britain for Hodder Education, an Hachette UK company,
338 Euston Road, London NW1 3BH, by Hobbs the Printers Ltd, Totton,
Hampshire SO40 3WX.

Contents

The Edinburgh Reading Tests

The **Edinburgh Reading Tests** form a series of standardised, semi-diagnostic tests for all school ages from 7:0 to 16+. They are primarily designed for administration to groups, although they can also be used with individuals. There are four tests in the series: **ERT1** for ages 7:0 to 9:0, **ERT2** for ages 8:6 to 10:6, **ERT3** for ages 10: to 12:6, and **ERT4** for ages 12:0 to 16:6.

Each test is divided into four or more subtests, each designed to assess a different area of reading competence, and is intended to be administered in two sessions of 25–50 minutes, including practice questions. For each pupil, the test yields an individual profile of strengths and weaknesses in reading, as well as a standardised score and Reading Age.

All four **Edinburgh Reading Tests** have been revised and updated in the years since their first publication, and have come to be regarded as synonymous with thoroughness and quality in school-based reading assessment. The most recent (2001/2) revision programme has enabled full updating, redesign and reorigination of the test booklets, and complete restandardisation of **ERT1–3**: most of the participating schools contributed data for **ERT 1, 2** and **3**, giving broad continuity throughout the primary phase. For **ERT4**, the age range of the test has been extended to 16:6.

THE PURPOSE OF THE TESTS

The construction of these tests was undertaken in the belief that instruments of this kind, designed for use by teachers and requiring no special psychometric expertise to administer or interpret results, can assist in the teaching of reading. Such tests can provide information that will help the teacher, whether organising group activities or attending to the special needs of an individual pupil. In the light of the test results she[1] can adapt teaching methods and choose teaching materials to remedy a weakness or build on a strength.

These tests are straightforward to administer and simple to mark, and will help the teacher to appreciate more clearly both the general attainment and the particular strengths and weaknesses of each pupil. They will also help the teacher to evaluate the success of her own teaching methods with respect to the whole or to special areas of reading.

It must be emphasised that the tests, while containing a wide variety of types of material, are *tests*, and should always be treated as such. They do not necessarily represent good *teaching* practice, and are not intended to be used as teaching material. In practice, teaching for the test is unlikely to be successful as no substantial difficulty is involved in coping with the item types. If it is successful, then it serves only to reduce the validity of the results. The test should be used only as part of a carefully planned system of assessment, diagnosis and appropriate follow-up.

For every pupil, the teacher can obtain an overall score for the whole test, and a separate score for each subtest. The **overall score** gives a valid and reliable estimate of a pupil's reading attainment, on the basis of the various aspects of reading sampled in the test. This score can be converted into a *standardised score* which relates the pupil's performance to that of the population and shows where the pupil stands in relation to other pupils of the same age. Each pupil's overall score can also be converted to a *Reading Age*.

Within each test, the **subtests** are aimed at measuring different aspects of reading competence relevant to the age range being tested. As a result, the subtests tend to be most relevant to pupils within the designated age range. Here the intention is not to compare the child with other children, but to make comparisons within the child's *own* performance. For example, a pupil aged 10 who has a nominal reading age of, say, 8, may well not encounter the same difficulties found by an average-ability eight-year-old taking the same test. Since they consist of fewer items, the subtests do not give as reliable results as the whole test, but they do give a useful diagnostic pointer to an individual pupil's areas of relative strength and weakness in reading. Small differences should therefore be disregarded, and a simple method is provided for showing which relatively high or low scores are worth

---

[1] For convenience and clarity, the teacher is referred to as 'she' and the pupil as 'he' throughout this manual.

taking note of. When a subtest score is picked out in this way, the teacher should not assume that it definitely indicates a strength or weakness, but should confirm the test's diagnosis through her own observations.

Detailed suggestions are made for the interpretation of the subtest scores and for work arising from them.

The ERT and the English National Curriculum

The National Curriculum Attainment Target for Reading is organised in levels, at each of which the expected attainment of pupils is described by a *Level Description*. Each of these Level Descriptions takes the form of a performance criterion defining an area of knowledge, skill and/or understanding. For the most part, these criteria are broadly defined, and the Attainment Target as a whole takes a wide view of development in reading. It encompasses not only the ability to read increasingly complex texts accurately and with understanding, but also, for instance, information retrieval strategies, awareness of the author's use of words, and the ability to respond to and talk about what has been read, expressing and justifying opinions and preferences. This is reinforced by the National Literacy Strategy.

Assessment of pupils' achievement in relation to these broad and varied criteria is necessarily different in many respects from that of the **ERT** and other standardised tests of reading. As group tests designed for relatively quick administration and scoring, the **ERT** are necessarily based on relatively brief and isolated activities and texts to which pupils respond in writing; National Curriculum assessments involve a wide range of whole texts to which pupils respond in a variety of different ways. The outcomes of the two are also different. National Curriculum assessment provides relatively coarse Level scores and descriptive information about what children can and cannot do; the **ERT** provide Reading Ages and finer, numerical scores which enable a pupil's achievement to be compared with a national average and with that of other pupils.

Despite these differences, there are ways in which the complementary assessment procedures can usefully be related. This is particularly the case at the level of the individual subtest scores provided by the **ERT**. The skills covered by these subtests represent aspects of development in reading which are not only significant in their own right, but

which can also be seen as underpinning and contributing to the more broadly defined areas in the Attainment Target for reading. Such parallels mean that the pattern of strengths and weaknesses revealed by the **ERT** subtests can throw light on a pupil's progression through National Curriculum levels of attainment. In particular, the more sharply focused **Edinburgh Reading Tests** provide information about some of the basic skills, without which the broader, more inclusive competencies described in the Attainment Target for reading cannot be achieved.

The ERT and the National Curriculum Guidelines in Scotland

The *Scottish National Guidelines for English Language* identify four broad areas of the language curriculum – Listening, Talking, Reading and Writing – termed *attainment outcomes*. Within each outcome there are described a number of *strands* or aspects of learning (e.g. listening in groups, talking about experiences, reading for information, personal writing). Most strands have attached to them statements of minimum competency or *attainment targets*, now at six broad levels of development covering primary and early secondary education from age 5 to 14 years.

Six strands, or aspects of learning, are defined for Reading:

- Reading for information
- Reading for enjoyment
- Reading to reflect on the writer's ideas and craft
- Awareness of genre (type of text)
- Reading aloud
- Knowledge about language

While there is no direct link between the **ERT** subtests and the reading strands and attainment targets set out in the 5–14 programme, the skills and competences covered by the tests represent important aspects of pupils' overall linguistic development. For example, a pupil cannot be expected to read regularly for enjoyment without the ability to read at a reasonable rate, to understand essential ideas, to use context as a guide to understanding and without having a suitable range of vocabulary. Thus, while the 5–14 English Language Guidelines describe what a pupil at different stages can be expected to do in terms of the Reading outcome, the **Edinburgh Reading Tests** assess some of the basic skills without which the desired outcome could not be achieved.

Edinburgh Reading Test 1

Edinburgh Reading Test 1 comes in two parallel forms: Form A (printed in brown ink) and Form B (blue ink). Each of these consists of four independent subtests, totalling 91 items:

Subtest A – Vocabulary *(20 items)*
Subtest B – Syntax *(30 items)*
Subtest C – Sequences *(20 items)*
Subtest D – Comprehension *(21 items)*

There are two principal reasons for the use of parallel forms:

- First, by removing the danger of a 'practice' effect that may result from repeated use of the same form, it enables teachers to monitor progress over time (most important at this age).
- Second, because children at this age are accustomed to working together (with no implication of 'cheating'), parallel forms can serve to reduce the amount of copying which might otherwise take place and which would obviously be inappropriate in the context of a test.

Therefore, the two forms are designed to be used simultaneously, and should be distributed so that each child has, on his left and on his right – and if necessary facing him – children doing the other form.

It is important to remember that, although one may elect to describe it as 'reading' or a 'workbook' to the children, the test is a test. Therefore we must not treat it as reading material and attempt to minimise errors, but give the children as much opportunity as possible to make the errors they make in their own unaided efforts. Neither, it must be said, do the items necessarily represent good teaching practice. They are intended to assess, rather than improve, children's performance.

Timing

It is recommended that, although all four subtests are contained in one booklet, the testing should occupy two sessions, in order to reduce fatigue. The recommended place for the break, which might be playtime or lunch, is at the end of page 7. It is preferable, but not essential, to complete administration in the course of one day. Timing for the individual sections is not exact, but no page should take more then three minutes to complete. Therefore, the whole test contains approximately 30 minutes' working time. Since there are no written instructions, however – all instructions being explained by the teacher – the total administration time is somewhat longer (approximately 25 minutes per session, depending on the class). Accuracy of timing is not crucial, but it is important not to give the children time to get bored, and the guidelines given in the instructions should therefore be adhered to.

Preparation

Each child will need a pencil or ball-point pen. Replacements should be kept readily available. Erasers may also be used. Errors may be crossed out or rubbed out. The children may like to colour the pictures when they have completed the test, but should not be offered the prospect in advance.

No other materials will be required. It is therefore helpful if the children clear their desks or tables before starting on the test.

The children should be seated in separate desks if at all feasible, as it will further help to reduce copying. However, this is very commonly impossible in primary school classrooms, and is not absolutely essential, due to the use of the parallel forms. Under no circumstances, however, should any children sitting next to each other at one table be given the same form. The main problem is not one of cheating, but of automatic collaboration. It is necessary to keep this, and the children's urge to ask the teacher to sort out problems, to a minimum. A second supervisor is desirable, but the test can be conducted by one person.

Giving the test

Distribute the question booklets. The pupils should not open the booklets at this stage. The section on the back page is for pupil information to be entered. Ask the children to enter the information. For increased accuracy, you may wish to fill in some of the information yourself after the scripts have been collected in (e.g. pupil age in years and months) at the same time as you are scoring the test.

The following instructions are not intended to be followed absolutely rigidly, but should be followed fairly closely. The purpose is to explain to the children, in as lively and interesting manner as possible, what they are being asked to do. Obviously the quick ones will grasp immediately what is required of them, but the slower ones, at whom these instructions and the test itself are aimed, may have more trouble. However, the ability level of the class as a whole should determine the tenor of administration.

FIRST SESSION

Before starting, write on the board the second example (page 3 in the test booklet), as follows:

A dog has four (tails / humps / noses / legs)

Underneath this, write the third example (page 4 in the test booklet):

Why are you been late?

Tell the children that they will be working individually through the test, and not to worry if they can't do a question, but just go on to the next. Hand out the booklets, telling the children not to open them. Tell them to write their names on the cover, if this has not already been done.

Say: "Open your books at the first page. It has some pictures on it (check that they are at the correct page). Do you see the picture of a dog? It is the first picture on the page. There are some words around it. Only one of those words says 'dog'. Put your finger on it. Have you got the right one? The word that says 'dog' is circled. Can you see that?

"What's the next picture on the page? (obtain the answer from the class). That's right, it's a tree. Now, I want you to find the word that says 'tree', and draw a circle round it (pause). Have you done that? Good. Now I want you to go on and do the same for all the other pictures. Find the word that says what the picture shows, and draw a circle around it. Remember, there are two pages of pictures for you to do. Do both pages."

After three minutes, or sooner if most of the children seem to have done all that they can, *say:*

"That's enough. Let's turn over and go on to the next page (*check that they are at the correct page*). I've written the first line on the board (*pointing*). 'A dog has four . . .' Four what? (*pointing to each word in turn*). Four tails? I don't think so. How about humps? Noses? A dog with four noses! (*pointing*). What a strange dog that would be! No, it must be legs (*pointing*). A dog has four legs. Is that right? Of course it is! So we circle 'legs' (*circle on the board*).

"Now, without speaking, I want you to do the same to the next sentence. 'Jo cooks in the . . .' Circle the word that says the place where Jo cooks (*pause*). Have you done this? Good. Now go on and do the same to all the others. Finish each sentence by drawing a circle around the right word."

After three minutes, or when most of the children seem to have done all that they can, *say:*

"That's enough, now. Let's go on to the next page. I've written the first line on the board. 'Why are you been late?' Can you see anything wrong with that? (*pause*). Yes, there is something wrong with it: 'been' isn't needed in this sentence; it doesn't belong at all. If we cross it out, the sentence is 'Why are you late?' which is good sense.

"Look at the next line and, without speaking, cross out the word that doesn't belong or isn't needed (*pause*). Have you done that? Good. Now, I want you to go on and do the same to all the rest. Cross out, in every sentence, the word that doesn't belong or isn't needed."

After three minutes, or when most of the children seem to have done all that they can, *say:*

"That's enough of that. Turn over to the next page (*check that they are at the correct page*). Look at the picture. It shows a lorry, and a woman and a boy. On the other page is a story, about the lorry and the woman and the boy. But there are some gaps in the story, and you have to fill them by circling the word that fits best in the gap.

"Look at the first line, 'one . . . day'. What kind

of day could it be? It was a sunny day. Like (or not like) today. That's why 'sunny' is circled. It's the word that goes in the space. What about the next part of the story, 'as John was . . . home'? Now, without speaking, I want you to go on and circle all the words that should be in the gaps, until the story is finished."

After three minutes, or when most of the children seem to have done all that they can, *say:*

"That's enough, now. Let's turn over and go on to page 7 (*check that they are at the correct page*). Look at the first line. Do you see what it says? 'Mum went out, and took David.' Underneath, there is a question for us to answer. Shall we try? 'Did David go out?' What do you think? Yes or No (*pause*). Yes, of course he did. If Mum went out, and took David, then David went out too, so 'yes' has been circled. Now, without speaking go on and answer the next question. Don't read it out, just circle the correct answer on the right. Don't go on to the next page yet. Just answer the questions on this page."

This is a convenient moment to take a break. If a break is taken, the booklets should obviously be collected, unless the room is certain to be undisturbed for the whole period of the break. In any case, the booklets should be left closed. Therefore, after three minutes, *say:* "That's enough for now. Put down your pencils, and close your books."

An interval of at least 15 minutes and at most 24 hours should elapse between the administration of the first and second sessions.

SECOND SESSION

Before starting, write on the board the example at the top of page 8. If necessary, redistribute the booklets, and make sure that each child has the correct one.

Say: "Everybody turn now to page 8 (*check that they are at the correct page*). I've written the first line on the board. Look at the first line: 'feet big children tall have.' What does that mean? (*pause*). You don't know? That's because it doesn't really mean anything! But imagine the words are on separate pieces of paper, so that we can move them around. Say we start with 'have' (*write the word on the board*). What word could go with 'have'? 'Children have' or 'feet have'? But if we say 'feet have', we must say 'feet have children', which is silly. So it must be (*writing*) 'children have (*leave gap*) feet'. Now, what are we left with? 'Big', and 'tall'. Both of these go with other words, because they say something about them. But 'tall' can't go with 'feet' – who has heard of 'tall feet'? So it must go with 'children': that makes the sentence 'tall children have big feet'. We draw a circle around 'tall', because it's the **first word** of the sentence we've made."

"Now, without speaking, do the same with the next one: make a proper sentence out of 'hungry . . . children . . . always...are' and just draw a circle around the word that **starts** your sentence (*pause*). Have you done that? Good. Now go on and do that with all the others. Make up a real sentence out of the words, and draw a circle around the **first** word."

After three minutes, or when most of the children seem to have done all they can, *say:*

"Let's turn over and go on to the next page (*check that they are all at the correct page*). Look at the first line: 'Would you like to play football with us?' It's a question, isn't it? Do you see the letter 'C' after it? If we look down to the lines with letters in front of them, we find the answer to the question: 'I can't, I've got to do my homework'. So we get: **Question:** 'Would you like to play football with us?' **Answer:** 'I can't, I've got to do my homework.' With the next line, 'How about tomorrow?', what is the answer? (*pause*). Don't tell me, just think to yourself. Now, can you tell me what letter that is? Write it on the line underneath the 'C'. Now I want you to put, after the other two questions, the letters of the right answers, just like the first two (*pause*). Have you done that? Good.

"Now, go and do exactly the same to the other two sets of questions on the next page. Put after them the letters that show which are the right answers."

After three minutes, or when most of the children seem to have done all that they can, *say:*

"Let's turn over and go on to the next page (*check that they are at the correct page*). Here we've got some pictures, and underneath some questions about the pictures. I want you to write the answers in the spaces. Do both sets of pictures." After three minutes, remind them to do both pages.

After six minutes, or when most of the children seem to have done all they can, *say:*

"Let's turn over to the next page. Look at the story you find there. It starts: 'When the bus broke down on the way to school, and they were told they had to wait for another one . . .' Now, look at the questions at the bottom. 'Who didn't want to be late?' Alice said 'Oh good! I don't want to go to school.' So it wasn't her, was it? But Billy said 'I hope this doesn't make me late.' So it was Billy who didn't want to be late, so Billy's name has been written in the space.

"Now, without speaking, I want you to answer the other two questions yourselves, by writing the name of the child who best answers that question (*pause*). Have you all done that? Good. Now let's go on to the other two stories on the next page. I want you to answer all the other questions in the same way. Be sure you do both pages."

After about three minutes, or when most of the children seem to have done all they can, *say:* "That's enough on that page. Close your books and hand them back to me."

Marking

- In marking, use only the official answer key given on the following pages.
- Before starting to mark, divide the scripts into Form A and Form B, and mark only one form at a time to avoid confusion.
- To make the task of marking as quick and easy as possible, and to ensure maximum accuracy, markers should deal with only one page at a time, and should make a point of repeating mentally only the correct answers when comparing key and script. The answers will thus be more quickly memorised.
- The answers are spaced according to the questions in the test. Marking is made easier if the test booklet is folded back and placed in the correct position alongside the answers in the key.
- Follow the answer key without deviation, even if occasionally some other answer seems plausible. In that case, or where an answer is not clear, draw attention to it by a note on the front cover.
- Award one mark for each correct answer; give no fractional marks.
- If the method of answering differs from that asked for in the rubric, or shown in the key (e.g. writing out an answer instead of circling it), give credit if the content of the answer is correct. If the child has changed his answer, by alteration or by crossing out and writing the answer at the side, give credit if the final intention is clear, and the content of the answer is correct.
- If more than one response is circled or otherwise marked (except by way of alteration) where only one should be, give no credit.
- On pages 11 and 12, the objective is to elicit the *appropriate* answer. Thus, some of the questions have more then one answer. The criterion is whether the response is one which is appropriate to the question. For example, page 11, question 1, in Form B, has several possible answers: 'letters', 'mail' or 'parcels' would be appropriate; 'the postman' or 'Royal Mail' would not. Similarly in Form A, page 11, question 7, 'dog', 'a dog' or 'fierce dog' are appropriate, but not 'beware of the dog'.
- The marks should be recorded on the page as it is marked, and totalled at the foot of each page. The page totals should then be transferred to the back cover of the test booklet (to the column headed 'Raw Score') and totalled, for each subtest and for the test as a whole.
- The child's age in years and months should be written on the back cover. This age should be given in years and completed months: for example, a child born on 16 March 1994 and tested on 15 April 2002 was aged 8:0.
- The back cover, when completed, can be removed and used as a record-sheet: it contains all the information likely to be gained, about most children, from the test. Do not, however, remove the back cover until any unusual profile characteristic has been investigated.

Note: A **Scorer/Profiler CD-ROM** is available to facilitate rapid, computerised conversion of pupils' subtest raw scores to standardised scores and reading ages, and to generate subtest profiles for each pupil as well as a range of class/group performance analyses.

Answers

PAGE 1

1. tree

2. teapot

3. bulldozer

4. train

PAGE 2

5. needle

6. girl

7. bucket

8. boat

9. knife

PAGE 3

1. kitchen

2. bread

3. fish

4. fruit

5. television

6. coat

7. wheels

8. sets

9. beach

10. fish

11. fortnight

PAGE 4

1. she
2. chair
3. eats
4. to
5. plays
6. for
7. kittens
8. with
9. far
10. who

PAGE 6

1. going
2. who
3. said
4. was
5. noisy
6. goes
7. driver
8. went
9. what
10. to

PAGE 7

1. no
2. John
3. David
4. the policeman
5. no
6. no
7. the man
8. Anshu
9. one
10. Ruth

Form A   Subtest C

PAGE 8	PAGE 9	PAGE 10
		4. B
		5. A
1. children	1. A	6. D
2. when	2. D	7. C
3. your	3. B	
4. how		
5. why		
6. when		
7. vegetables		8. B
8. tell		9. D
9. can		10. A
		11. C

In this section, do not penalise the children if the answer is correct, but incorrectly spelled, or phrased slightly differently. Do not, however, allow responses (such as 'beware of the dog' for p. 11, q. 4) which are not correct 'in spirit'.

PAGE 11	PAGE 12	PAGE 13	PAGE 14
			3. Derek
			4. Alex
			5. Claire
1. Foxhill			
	1. 2		
2. Star			
3. flowers, plants	2. 7.30 (half past seven)		
4. litter, waste paper	3. yes		
5. Old Street	4. yes	1. David	
			6. Brian
6. Green	5. yes	2. Alice	7. Dick
7. a dog	6. no		8. Alan

PAGE 1

1. tree

2. snake

3. chair

4. tent

PAGE 2

5. ladder

6. tractor

7. bed

8. parachute

9. fountain

PAGE 3

1. kitchen

2. flower

3. wool

4. library

5. forget

6. classroom

7. cook

8. teeth

9. station

10. bonfires

11. medicine

Form B

Subtest B

PAGE 4

1. heavy
2. off
3. out
4. these
5. nose
6. away
7. to
8. give
9. milk
10. breakfast

PAGE 6

1. going
2. met
3. lived
4. carry
5. shopping
6. saw
7. because
8. slower
9. did
10. how

PAGE 7

1. June
2. John
3. no
4. the man
5. Sara
6. no
7. Sam
8. the man
9. one
10. John

PAGE 8	PAGE 9	PAGE 10
		4. B
		5. D
1. children	1. A	6. A
2. Peter	2. D	7. C
3. I	2. B	
4. my		
5. teach		
6. who		
7. teacher		
8. we		8. D
9. I'll		9. B
		10. A
		11. C

In this section, do not penalise the children if the answer is correct, but incorrectly spelled, or phrased slightly differently. Do not, however, allow responses (such as 'postman' for p. 11, q. 1) which are not correct 'in spirit'.

PAGE 11	PAGE 12	PAGE 13	PAGE 14
			3. Cathy
			4. Bobby
			5. Debbie
1. letters, parcels, mail, post (*not* Royal Mail)			
2. Florist, Flower (shop)	1. No. 14		
3. no (it's open)	2. No. 33		
4. High Street	3. No. N1	1. David	
5. at the Bus Stop	4. no	2. Alice	6. Colin
6. Stop	5. 15 minutes		7. Anne
7. Circus	6. No. N1		8. Barry

Total Scores: Standardised Scores and Percentiles

The standardised scores, reading ages and subtest profiles described on the following pages can all be computer-generated using a *Scorer/Profiler CD-ROM*, available separately from the publishers. Teachers are nevertheless strongly advised to read these pages in order to understand fully what the different types of scores mean and how to interpret them.

Calculation and interpretation of total scores

The total scores, obtained by adding together all the correct responses, are in some ways inadequate to provide clear information about the child's performance. Firstly, they do not relate the performance to any well-defined standard and, secondly, they do not make any allowance for age. For these reasons, it is desirable to convert the 'raw' obtained scores to **standardised scores**: scores which do indicate how well a child has performed relative to a given population and, in particular, to others of the same age. A conversion table (Table 1), which applies both to Scotland and to England, is provided for this test, on pages 20–1; it is based on the performance of children in schools in various parts of the UK. (For details of the standardisation sample, see page 30.)

In **Table 1**, raw scores are set against ages in years and completed months. A child's standardised score is the number at the intersection of the line for his total raw score with the column for his age. Find a child's total score, therefore, in the left-hand margin of the appropriate table, and look along the row to the number appearing in the column for his age. For example, a child with a total score of 75 and an age of 7:2 has a standardised score of 104.

The standardised score is easily recorded for each child. Reading his total score and age from the back cover of the test booklet, follow the procedure described above and write the standardised score in the place provided. These standardised scores indicate how well a child has done by relating his performance to that of other children of the same age. Technically, they are normally distributed with a mean of 100 and a standard deviation of 15; but it is best to interpret them as showing what percentage of children, from the standardisation sample, obtained a score no higher. Thus a standardised score of 100 indicates that just 50% of children of the same age did no better. Similarly, a standardised score of 75 indicates that only 5% of children of the same age did no better.

Table 2 gives the approximate percentages corresponding to different standardised scores.

It may be wondered why these **percentiles** should not be given directly in place of the standardised scores. The standardised scores are used, however, with the intention that the results should be distributed according to what is reasonably supposed to be the actual distribution of (presently realised) ability. It will be seen that most children obtain standardised scores fairly close to 100, 50% of them between 90 and 110, while far fewer children obtain scores at either extreme. This corresponds to the common observation that most people are of much the same ability, while only a few are very bright or very dull. The use of standardised scores is intended to ensure that a difference of one point should roughly represent a constant difference in ability at whatever level of score or ability it occurs.

Table 1 Standardised Scores

AGE IN YEARS AND COMPLETED MONTHS AT DATE OF TEST

(Blank cells in the upper-left area carry the instruction: **AWARD 130+ FOR ALL SCORES IN THIS AREA**)

Raw score	7:0	7:1	7:2	7:3	7:4	7:5	7:6	7:7	7:8	7:9	7:10	7:11	8:0	8:1	8:2	8:3	8:4	8:5	8:6	8:7	8:8	8:9	8:10	8:11	9:0	Raw score
91									130	130	130	130	130	130	130	130	130	130	130	130	130	130	130	130	130	91
90								130	130	130	130	130	130	130	130	130	130	130	130	129	128	127	126	125	124	90
89							130	130	130	130	130	130	129	128	128	127	126	125	124	123	122	121	120	119	118	89
88						130	129	128	127	126	125	125	124	123	123	122	121	120	119	118	117	116	115	114	113	88
87					130	129	127	126	125	123	122	121	120	119	118	118	117	116	115	114	113	113	111	110	109	87
86				130	129	127	126	124	123	121	120	119	117	116	115	115	114	113	112	111	110	109	108	106	104	86
85			130	128	127	125	124	122	120	118	117	115	114	113	112	112	111	110	109	108	107	106	104	102	100	85
84		130	128	126	125	123	121	119	117	115	114	112	111	111	110	109	108	108	107	105	104	103	101	99	95	84
83	120	119	118	117	116	115	114	113	112	111	110	109	109	109	108	107	106	105	104	103	102	100	98	96	94	83
82	116	115	114	113	112	111	111	110	110	109	109	108	108	107	106	105	104	104	102	101	100	98	96	94	93	82
81	113	112	111	110	110	109	109	109	108	107	107	106	106	105	104	104	103	102	101	99	98	96	94	93	92	81
80	111	110	110	109	109	108	108	108	107	106	106	105	104	104	103	102	101	100	99	98	96	95	93	92	91	80
79	109	109	109	108	108	107	107	106	106	105	104	104	103	102	102	101	100	99	98	96	95	94	93	91	90	79
78	108	108	108	107	107	106	106	105	104	104	103	103	102	101	100	99	99	97	96	95	94	93	92	90	89	78
77	107	107	106	106	105	105	104	104	103	103	102	102	101	100	99	98	97	96	95	94	93	92	91	90	89	77
76	106	106	105	105	104	104	104	103	103	102	101	100	100	99	98	97	97	95	94	93	92	91	90	89	88	76
75	105	105	104	104	104	103	103	102	102	101	100	100	99	98	97	96	96	94	93	93	91	90	89	89	88	75
74	105	104	104	103	103	102	102	101	101	100	99	99	98	97	96	95	95	94	93	92	91	90	89	88	88	74
73	104	104	103	103	102	101	101	100	100	99	99	98	97	96	95	95	94	93	92	91	90	89	89	88	87	73
72	103	103	102	102	101	101	100	100	99	98	98	97	96	95	95	94	93	92	91	90	89	89	88	87	87	72
71	102	103	101	101	100	100	99	99	98	98	97	96	95	95	94	93	92	92	91	90	89	88	88	87	86	71
70	102	102	101	101	100	99	99	98	98	97	96	96	95	94	93	93	92	91	90	89	89	88	87	86	86	70
69	101	100	100	100	99	99	98	98	97	96	96	95	94	94	93	92	91	90	90	89	88	87	87	86	85	69
68	100	100	99	99	99	98	98	97	96	96	95	94	94	93	92	91	91	90	89	88	88	87	86	86	85	68
67	100	99	99	99	98	98	97	96	96	95	94	94	93	92	92	91	90	89	89	88	87	87	86	85	85	67
66	99	99	98	98	97	97	96	96	95	94	94	93	93	92	91	90	90	89	88	88	87	86	85	85	84	66
65	98	98	98	97	97	96	96	95	95	94	93	92	92	91	91	90	89	89	88	87	86	85	85	84	84	65
64	98	98	97	97	96	96	95	95	94	93	93	92	92	91	90	89	89	88	87	87	86	85	85	84	84	64
63	97	97	97	96	96	95	95	94	93	93	92	92	91	90	90	89	88	88	87	86	86	85	84	84	83	63
62	97	97	96	96	95	95	94	94	93	92	92	91	91	90	89	89	88	87	87	86	85	84	84	84	83	62
61	96	96	96	95	95	94	94	93	93	92	91	91	90	89	89	88	88	87	86	85	85	84	84	83	83	61
60	96	96	95	95	94	94	93	93	92	92	91	90	90	89	88	88	87	86	86	85	84	84	83	83	82	60
59	96	95	95	94	94	94	93	92	92	91	91	90	89	89	88	87	87	86	85	85	84	84	83	83	82	59
58	95	95	95	94	94	93	93	92	91	91	90	89	89	88	88	87	86	86	85	84	84	83	83	82	82	58
57	95	95	94	94	93	93	92	92	91	90	90	89	89	88	87	87	86	85	85	84	84	83	83	82	82	57
56	95	94	94	93	93	92	92	91	91	90	89	89	88	88	87	86	86	85	84	84	83	83	82	82	81	56
55	94	94	93	93	92	92	91	91	90	90	89	88	88	87	87	86	85	85	84	83	83	82	82	81	81	55
54	94	93	93	92	92	91	91	90	90	89	89	88	87	87	86	86	85	84	84	83	82	82	82	81	81	54
53	94	93	92	92	91	91	90	90	89	89	88	87	87	86	86	85	84	84	83	82	82	81	81	81	80	53
52	93	92	92	91	91	90	90	89	89	88	88	87	87	86	85	85	84	83	83	82	82	81	81	81	80	52
51	93	92	91	91	91	90	89	89	89	88	87	87	86	86	85	84	84	83	83	82	82	81	81	80	80	51
50	93	92	91	91	90	90	89	89	88	88	87	87	86	85	85	84	83	83	82	82	81	81	80	80	80	50
	7:0	7:1	7:2	7:3	7:4	7:5	7:6	7:7	7:8	7:9	7:10	7:11	8:0	8:1	8:2	8:3	8:4	8:5	8:6	8:7	8:8	8:9	8:10	8:11	9:0	

AGE IN YEARS AND COMPLETED MONTHS AT DATE OF TEST

AWARD 70 — FOR ALL SCORES IN THIS AREA

Raw score	9:0	8:11	8:10	8:9	8:8	8:7	8:6	8:5	8:4	8:3	8:2	8:1	8:0	7:11	7:10	7:9	7:8	7:7	7:6	7:5	7:4	7:3	7:2	7:1	7:0	Raw score
49	79	80	80	80	81	81	82	82	83	84	84	85	86	86	87	87	88	89	89	90	90	91	91	92	92	49
48	79	79	80	80	81	81	82	82	83	83	84	84	85	86	86	87	88	88	89	89	90	90	91	91	92	48
47	79	79	79	80	80	81	81	82	82	83	83	84	85	85	86	87	87	88	88	89	89	90	90	91	92	47
46	78	79	79	79	80	80	81	81	82	82	83	84	84	85	86	86	87	87	88	89	89	90	90	91	91	46
45	78	79	79	79	80	80	81	81	82	82	83	83	84	85	85	86	86	87	87	88	89	90	90	90	91	45
44	78	78	78	78	79	79	80	80	81	81	82	83	84	84	85	86	86	87	87	88	88	89	89	90	90	44
43	77	78	78	78	79	79	80	80	81	81	82	82	83	84	84	85	86	86	87	88	88	89	89	90	90	43
42	77	77	78	78	78	79	79	80	80	81	81	82	83	83	84	85	85	86	87	87	87	88	89	89	90	42
41	77	77	77	78	78	79	79	80	80	81	81	82	82	83	84	84	85	86	86	87	87	88	88	89	89	41
40	76	77	77	77	78	78	79	79	80	80	81	81	82	83	83	84	85	85	86	87	87	88	88	89	89	40
39	76	76	77	77	77	78	78	79	79	80	80	81	81	82	83	83	84	85	86	86	87	87	88	88	89	39
38	76	76	76	77	77	77	78	78	79	79	80	80	81	82	82	83	84	85	85	86	86	87	88	88	89	38
37	75	76	76	76	77	77	77	78	78	79	79	80	81	81	82	83	83	84	85	86	86	87	87	88	88	37
36	75	75	75	76	76	77	77	77	78	78	79	80	80	81	81	82	83	84	84	85	86	86	87	87	88	36
35	74	75	75	75	76	76	77	77	77	78	79	79	80	80	81	82	82	83	84	85	85	86	87	87	88	35
34	74	74	75	75	75	75	76	77	77	78	78	79	79	80	80	81	82	83	83	84	85	86	86	87	87	34
33	73	74	74	75	75	75	76	76	77	77	78	78	79	79	80	81	81	82	83	84	85	85	86	86	87	33
32	73	73	74	74	74	74	75	76	76	77	77	78	78	79	79	80	81	82	82	83	84	85	86	86	87	32
31	72	73	73	73	74	74	75	75	76	76	77	77	78	78	79	80	80	81	82	83	84	84	85	86	86	31
30	72	72	73	73	73	74	74	75	75	76	76	77	77	78	78	79	80	81	81	82	83	84	85	86	86	30
29	71	72	72	73	73	73	74	74	75	75	76	76	77	77	78	78	79	80	81	82	82	83	84	85	86	29
28	71	71	72	72	72	73	73	74	74	75	75	76	76	77	77	78	79	79	80	81	82	83	84	85	85	28
27	71	71	71	71	72	72	73	73	74	74	75	75	76	76	77	77	78	79	80	80	81	82	83	84	85	27
26	70	70	71	71	71	72	72	72	73	73	74	74	75	76	76	77	77	78	79	80	81	82	82	83	85	26
25	70	70	70	70	71	71	71	72	72	73	73	74	74	75	75	76	77	77	78	79	80	81	82	83	84	25
24			70	70	70	71	71	71	72	72	73	73	74	74	75	75	76	77	77	78	79	80	81	82	83	24
23					70	70	70	71	72	72	72	73	73	74	74	75	75	76	77	78	78	80	80	81	82	23
22							70	70	71	71	72	72	73	73	73	74	74	75	76	77	78	79	80	81	82	22
21								70	70	71	71	72	72	73	72	73	73	74	75	76	77	78	79	80	81	21
20									70	70	70	71	71	71	72	72		74	74	75	76	77	78	79	80	20
19												70	70	70	71	71	72	73	73	74	75	76	77	78	79	19
18														70	70	71	71	72	72	73	74	75	76	77	78	18
17															70	70	70	71	71	72	73	74	75	76	77	17
16																	70	70	70	71	72	72	73	75	76	16
15																			70	70	71	71	72	73	74	15
14																					70	70	71	72	73	14
13																							70	71	71	13
12																								70	70	12
11																								70		11
10																										10
	9:0	8:11	8:10	8:9	8:8	8:7	8:6	8:5	8:4	8:3	8:2	8:1	8:0	7:11	7:10	7:9	7:8	7:7	7:6	7:5	7:4	7:3	7:2	7:1	7:0	

Stand. score	70	71	72	73	74	75	76	77	78	79	80	81
Percentile	2	3	3	4	4	5	5	6	7	8	9	10
Stand. score	82	83	84	85	86	87	88	89	90	91	92	93
Percentile	12	13	14	16	18	20	21	23	25	27	30	32
Stand. score	94	95	96	97	98	99	100	101	102	103	104	105
Percentile	34	37	39	42	44	47	50	53	56	58	61	63
Stand. score	106	107	108	109	110	111	112	113	114	115	116	117
Percentile	66	68	70	73	75	77	79	80	82	84	86	87
Stand. score	118	119	120	121	122	123	124	125	126	127	128	129
Percentile	88	90	91	92	93	94	95	95	96	96	97	97

Table 2   Age-adjusted percentiles for each standardised score

CAUTIONS

The standardised score a child receives measures his general reading performance at the time that the test is administered. It is based on his performance in the various tasks included in the test which sample different aspects of his present reading ability. The standardised score does *not* indicate a child's *potential* capacity for reading, and it sets no limits to his possible improvement. A low standardised score is a challenge to the teacher, a high standardised score an encouragement; neither prophesies the future with certainty.

The scores from all tests are liable to error. Much the most reliable results from the present test are those for the whole test; but, even here, some allowance must be made. It is probable that a child's 'true' standardised score is slightly closer to 100 than is the one he actually obtains, so that a high standardised score is probably an over-estimate and a low standardised score an under-estimate. But, on the average, there is a two-thirds chance that the child's true standardised score lies within plus or minus 3 points of the one he actually obtains and a 95% chance that it lies within plus or minus 6 points.

Interpreted in relation to the whole population, high and low standardised scores are likely to be exaggerated for a further reason. The test was standardised in ordinary classes in state primary schools. But schools in the independent sector may well contain a higher proportion of very good readers, so a high standardised score probably *over*-estimates a child's performance in relation to the total school population, state and private. On the other hand, the exclusion of special schools and remedial classes must lead to a low standardised score *under*-estimating a child's general standing.

The inability of the test to give accurate measurements above and below certain points is reflected in the curtailment of standardised scores above 130 and below 70. Standardised scores outside this range are not reliable enough to merit precise reporting; they simply mean that the child's attainment was outside the range of attainments which the test was designed to assess. In particular, a group test is not suitable for determining a child's needs for special education. All children not qualifying for a standardised score of 70 should therefore be recorded as having obtained 70−; but this should be taken as a recommendation for individual testing, by an educational psychologist, and not as an ultimate judgement of the child's serious backwardness in reading.

Finally, it must be recognised that any table of standardised scores relates a child's performance to that of a particular sample of children. Care was taken in the selection of samples for this standardisation to get as fair as possible a representation of the state school population. Clearly the results are likely to fit other populations less well. Changes in reading standards over time may also gradually render the standardisation inaccurate.

Reading Ages

The standardised scores and percentiles from Tables 1 and 2 relate a child's performance to that of others of the same age. Another way of placing a child's performance is to relate it to the age at which such a performance is typical. This is the method of **reading ages**. A child's reading age indicates that he is reading as well as the average child of that age.

The reading ages in **Table 3** were obtained by finding the middle score for each age group; for example, when the scores of all the children aged 7:5 were listed, the middle score was 71. Thus any pupil, whatever his actual age, who scores 71 is said to have a reading age equal to 7:5.

A limiting factor in providing reading ages is the need to test children outside the age-range for which the test is really intended. Only then can they be calculated for the brighter older child or the less bright younger one. But in the present standardisation, very few children tested were outside the age-range 7:0 to 9:0, and even these were atypical (i.e. of unusually low or high achievement for their ages). However, it is reasonable to assume that the relationship between age and raw score is linear and that this relationship continues to hold good outside the age range covered by the standardisation sample. With caution therefore, reading ages can be extrapolated *downwards* from 7:0. They cannot however be extrapolated upwards, from 9:0, due to a high degree of 'bunching' which occurred towards the top end of the mark scale. In Table 3, the extrapolated scores are given in italics.

Raw score	*61*	*62*	*63*	*64*	*65*	*66*	*67*	*68*	*69*
Reading age	*6:3*	*6:4*	*6:6*	*6:7*	*6:8*	*6:10*	*6:11*	*7:0*	*7:2*
Raw score	70	71	72	73	74	75	76	77	78
Reading age	7:3	7:4	7:6	7:7	7:9	7:10	7:11	8:1	8:2
Raw score	79	80	81	82	83	84	85		
Reading age	8:4	8:5	8:6	8:8	8:9	8:10	9:0		

Table 3   Reading Ages

The Subtests

Each section of the test constitutes a subtest intended to measure a particular aspect of reading competence. Section, or subtest, scores are awarded to a child only so that comparisons can be made between different aspects of his *own* performance. These scores are not intended to facilitate comparison of his performance with that of other children.

Testing is inherently an imprecise procedure and small variations between a given child's score on the various subtests are not necessarily significant. To help in the interpretation of the subtest scores, therefore, there is also a simple method of identifying which, if any, of a child's subtest scores are sufficiently high or low, relative to the others, to indicate that there may be special strengths or weaknesses for that subtest. This can be determined by reference to **Table 4**.

First locate the appropriate row in the table by finding in the first column the pupil's total raw score on the whole test. The other entries in that row give the range of raw scores for each subtest which would be expected for a pupil with a whole test score in that range. A subtest score outside the range can be regarded as unusually high or low, and should be noted in the score panel on the cover of the pupil's test booklet (tick *high* or *low*, as appropriate).

It will be noted that Table 4 does not cover

total raw scores of less than 15. This is because unusually low subtest scores are not possible for pupils whose whole test scores are as low as this, since their expected subtest scores are too low. Conversely, unusually high scores are not possible since they have not gained enough marks overall to have exceptionally high scores for any subtest.

These subtest results are not so reliable as the result for the whole test, because they are based on a smaller number of items. Great caution must be taken in their interpretation, therefore. Small differences between a pupil's scores on the different subtests may well arise by chance. Significance should not, therefore, be attached to every discrepancy.

When a subtest result is singled out as unusually high or low, the test is suggesting that this aspect of the pupil's ability should be looked at; but, even here, the teacher should not automatically accept the diagnosis, but should confirm it through her own observations. Also, the fact that a particular subtest score is singled out in this way does *not* mean that the teacher should pay no attention to the other results. The pattern of results may well suggest a meaningful interpretation of the pupil's difficulties in reading; but the pattern must not force an interpretation – as explained above, it may have arisen by chance.

Score on whole test	Subtest A range	Subtest B range	Subtest C range	Subtest D range
15–19	4–10	1–10	0–7	0–5
20–24	5–11	3–11	0–8	0–6
25–29	6–12	5–13	1–10	0–7
30–34	7–13	6–14	2–11	1–9
35–39	8–14	8–16	3–12	2–10
40–44	9–15	10–18	4–13	4–11
45–49	10–16	11–19	6–14	5–13
50–54	11–17	13–21	7–15	6–14
55–59	12–18	15–23	8–16	8–15
60–64	13–19	16–24	9–18	9–16
65–69	13–20	18–26	10–19	10–18
70–74	14–20	19–28	11–20	11–19
75–79	15–20	21–29	13–20	13–20
80–84	16–20	23–30	14–20	14–21
85–91	17–20	24–30	15–20	15–21

Table 4   Expected subtest scores for each whole test score.

Design and Interpretation of the Subtests

The general principle on which each subtest is constructed is that of isolating as far as possible the aspect of reading competence which it is supposed to test. Thus each subtest has been made as easy as it could be in all dimensions except the one with which it is concerned.

It might be expected, therefore, that the subtests would give markedly different assessments of a child, crediting him with distinctly greater competence in some aspects of reading than in others. The truth, however, with these subtests as with all other reading tests, is that they agree closely with each other about almost every child – that is, the subtests are highly correlated.

This means that reading can be thought of as a unified ability – an accomplishment which children tend to be good or bad at as a whole. Any abilities that we may distinguish within reading are interdependent; for, in any ordinary reading task, they are called upon in combination. Therefore, one aspect of reading skill is not likely to flourish without the others.

The **ERT1** subtests keep four of these aspects – vocabulary, syntax, sequences and comprehension – as far apart as possible, but the differences to be found in this way are in most cases small and educationally insignificant. Most children need help right across the board, and not in one ability more than in any other.

The warning against placing weight on every discrepancy does not, therefore, have educationally undesirable consequences. The subtests can, through their separation of tasks, pick out children who do need special help in particular skills; and the procedure is not likely to underestimate the relatively small number of children needing special, as well as general, assistance.

Note that in discussing the subtests, the emphasis has so far been placed on the diagnosis of abilities or disabilities that stand out from a child's general level of performance. Most children, however, as stated above, have all their abilities at much the same level. They include children who are weak in reading, whatever aspect is considered. **These children need help with every skill to the same degree as others need help on their one weakness.** The suggestions that follow for support work on the subtests should all be taken to apply to children who are backward on reading as a whole.

Low scores on the subtests

> **This section applies both to scores that are straightforwardly low, as well as to scores that are picked out on a child's profile as unusually low in the context of his general standard of performance.**

Given either type of low score, see first whether the child has misunderstood the structure of the items or the form of response required. Careful presentation of the practice items should have minimised misunderstanding of this nature; if it does occur, however, the poor result should be treated with caution.

Determine also whether the low score is a result of the child's not having attempted many items. If his other scores are good, his slowness may be due to a specific reaction to the subtest items. If, however, his other scores are low, it is extremely probable that the child's slowness does indicate that he is weak in the relevant skill. Indeed, it is possible that his more basic skills are not sufficiently developed for a meaningful assessment to be made of the ability that the subtest seeks to measure.

Each child found to have an unusually low score on any subtest should be seen individually by the teacher, who should discuss the subtest with him at a time when she is free to give him her full attention. Quite as much individual attention should be devoted to each child who has done poorly on the *whole* test (that is, at the very least, any child with a standardised score of 85 or less). Though the teacher may not have time to go through all the subtests with him, particularly if her class contains several such children, this would be the most desirable and advantageous course of action.

The teacher's explicit aim must be to 'find out what he found difficult', and there must be no hint of criticism. Otherwise a child will become defensive and valuable diagnostic information will be lost.

Sit down with the child, giving him a blank copy of the test open at a subtest on which he did badly. If this subtest result was exceptional for him, tell him that he did very well on most parts of the test; if he has done poorly throughout the test, reassure him that you are pleased with the way that he tackled the test. Then say that you want to go over this part of the test with him.

Ask him first whether he found it difficult. If he says 'No', give him a minute or two to recall the section and then see whether he can show you any parts that were difficult.

Get him to answer the subtest items, asking him to read them aloud and noting any errors in his reading. Notice if he is following the instructions correctly and, if not, explain them to him at this point. If he is very slow, try to find out what is puzzling him. If he gets an answer wrong, ask him why he thinks his answer is right.

Look for failure not only in the sub-skill being tested but also in word recognition and in keeping a grasp on the nature of the task. This will show whether the child is deficient in the sub-skill, or whether some other feature of this particular set of items caused him difficulty.

The individual subtests

The detailed notes that follow provide an analysis of the items in each subtest and suggest interpretations of unusually low and unusually high scores. Some teaching points are indicated in the 'rationale' sections for each subtest, though these are, of course, only a few of the many that will suggest themselves to teachers.

Subtest A: Vocabulary

The rationale of the items
Pages 1–2: A test of general vocabulary, intended to be within the power of all but the very poorest readers. These items discriminate best in the bottom third of the ability range. The distractors are intended to reveal:

(a) failure to read the whole word – 'tend' for 'tent', 'buckle' for 'bucket', 'chase' for 'chair', 'tress' for 'tree'.
(b) tendency to go on shape of word, and ignore individual letters -'boot' for 'boat', 'test' for 'tent', 'tram' for 'train'.
(c) accepting a similar sound – 'shake' for 'snake', 'drain' for 'train', 'stair' for 'chair'.

Any child having difficulty with these words is undoubtedly a very poor reader. Since the items contain no grammar or syntax, it may be that the child is still having trouble decoding individual words, and, if several of the wrong answers are of one of the types given above, this may be an indication that the child is experiencing a particular difficulty. Such children are probably in need of remedial attention, and therefore should be assessed individually; but working with objects and their names may well be helpful.

Page 3: Sentence completion, with the grammatical and syntactical content of the sentences as simple as possible. The child has to select the most appropriate word to complete the sentence. These items test:

(a) the ability to form categories (Form A, nos. 4 and 10; Form B, no. 2).
(b) the ability to connect occupation with essential features (Form A, no. 3; Form B, nos. 4 and 8).
(c) the ability to work out the essential attributes of an object.

For the rest, the sentences form a rule-of-thumb definition of one of the alternatives given.

Some of the distractors are based on simple misunderstandings of key words ('weeks' – 'strong'; 'dentist' – 'dents'; 'watch' – 'clothes') or alternative uses of them ('catch' – 'police' or 'nets'; 'take' – 'trouble'). Alternatively, mistakes may arise from picking out a key word – such as 'ill' – and associating it with a superficially plausible distractor – 'doctors'. At the simplest level, a few distractors still rely on shape – 'beards' for 'bread', 'knitting' for 'kitchen'.

The vocabulary of this page is put into context. It is therefore 'vocabulary' not in the sense of a simple matching of word to object or meaning, but that of selecting the appropriate word to express or complete a concept, or summarise the meaning of a phrase, albeit at a simple level.

Unusually low scores
An unusually low score on this subtest suggests a child who, although coming to terms with the structures of written language, and able to organise both words and constructions, is comparatively deficient in the recognition or understanding of individual words. If the shortfall is on page 3, it is likely that this deficiency is slightly beyond the simple word-recognition stage, and that specific drilling is unlikely to be very successful. It is more important to check that the child is

manipulating the words he already has, and is, for example, able to form categories, describe objects' attributes and uses, and connect together related activities, perhaps by writing about daily life, and discussing what he has written.

Unusually high scores
An unusually high score, while encouraging, is less likely to suggest a child with a rich vocabulary, than one whose satisfactory vocabulary is held back by difficulties in other areas. Attention should therefore be directed particularly to those areas in which the child scored below the median. In short, it is as well to treat a high score on this subtest as indicative of possible problems elsewhere. It may well be, however, that, although the child is having trouble with written syntax, for example, his vocabulary is sufficiently developed to allow him to cope with a wide range of material.

Subtest B: Syntax

The rationale of the items
This subtest includes three groups of items which, although they do not hang together in any especially coherent way, all cover the problems which develop when a child is in the process of making the transition from spoken to written language.

Page 4: This page tests the child's ability to discern the whole structure of the sentence, by means of the clues provided by the sentence structure to eliminate the word which is not only redundant, but positively distorting. There are three basic categories:

(a) words which are obviously inappropriate as soon as one comes to them (Form A, no. 2; Form B, no. 2).
(b) words whose inappropriateness is apparent only after one has read several more words.
(c) words at the beginning or end of the sentence, simulating a misplaced or omitted full stop.

This item type is more remote than any other from a desired reading behaviour, although it is a very satisfactory test. It cannot, therefore, be said to resemble a teaching tool in any way.

Page 6: This page is ordered as a story to provide more clues in a concise form. It could be described as a modified 'cloze' test. It covers two main areas:

(a) the selection of the most suitable transformation from those offered.
(b) the selection of the most appropriate structure-word from those offered.

Most of the distractors for each 'type a' question are derived from a single root; those for 'type b' questions represent a combination of non-standard usage (possible in spoken, but not written English) and words which, although wholly inappropriate, are of similar type.

Page 7: The central theme of page 7 is the complexity of written English idiom, and specific elements which may create difficulty in making the transition from spoken to written English. It covers such areas as passives, reported speech, adjectival clauses, and the use of 'neither . . . nor' and 'both . . . and'. The distractors are relatively simple, and many of the questions are of the yes/no type. Too much cannot therefore be read into answers.

Unusually low scores
The material contained in this subtest taps an area which is crucial to the transition from spoken to written English. Written English has its own standards, and there are many forms peculiar to it. Unless a child can come to terms with this, he will never be happy with reading, for a large proportion of the cues available in speech – such as inflections, facial expressions, and the immediate rephrasing of an obscure word or phrase – are absent from written speech or expressed as new, graphic, signals. In its turn, written language has an inflexibility, and obscurity, all its own. The child has to learn, when he has passed beyond simple decoding, new ways of putting words together, and a rigidity of form which is absent from spoken English.

It may be helpful to ascertain in which group of items the difficulty is most apparent. Thus, if page 4 presents special difficulty, the child is failing to see a sentence as a coherent group of words, with its own organisation which excludes a surplus word. If he is having difficulty with page 6, there are two basic areas where the trouble may lie: in making the transformations of roots to appropriate forms, or in appreciating the need for a particular structure-word. It may be helpful to go through the page, noting in which group (if either) the errors particularly fall. On page 7, the distance the child progresses may be crucial. The early part of the page is concerned with simple structures, such as passives, 'neither ... nor', and adjectival clauses. The latter part is made up of reported speech, where the child's handling of a system of graphic signals which should be known to him is tested. Clearly, the child who is failing over reported speech is in a very different category from one who has not yet grasped the essential coherence of a sentence. It is, however, worth ascertaining, for example in discussion, how well the child has grasped the essential concepts of print. If this is satisfactory, it may be that the child is not yet at home with written syntax, and requires extensive practice in, and discussion of, the special features of written, as distinct from spoken, English.

Unusually high scores
A child scoring exceptionally highly on this subtest has probably come to grips with the basic problems of written English, and is therefore on the way to success in reading. However, if the other subtest scores are low, and the syntax score is therefore high only by comparison, attention should of course be paid to the child's deficiencies.

Subtest C: Sequences

The rationale of the items
Concepts of sequence are essential to reading at any level, from the orientation and sequencing of letters into words, and the sequencing of words, phrases and clauses, to the logical sequence of connected writing. It is therefore clearly necessary to check that the child has a grasp of sequential factors necessary to his stage of development.

Page 8: The items on this page test the child's ability to extract the appropriate word-order of sentences of varying degrees of complexity, from the simple verb-subject-object through a variety of relative clauses and questions. Although it would be less ambiguous to ask the child to put all the words in order, that would have been a very demanding task, and would have caused many problems for the least able children. Therefore, they are asked merely to pick out the *first* word of the sentences.

Pages 9–10: This group of items tests the child's ability to order a sequence of questions and answers, and therefore, it is hoped, to grasp the logical order of a paragraph of prose. The question-and-answer form was chosen in preference to that of a jumbled sequence of sentences as being simpler for the children to grasp. It is more logical to find a question requiring an answer than a statement requiring another statement to be connected with it. As a result, the indirectness of the exercise – a

problem which always plagues sequencing tests – is reduced. There is a gradient of difficulty introduced into the latter two groups by increasing similarity in form of the answers, and the relatively greater plausibility of more than one answer to the latter questions.

Unusually low scores
Some interdependence of subtests B and C, due to the fact that syntactical and grammatical clues are essential to sequencing, is unavoidable. On pages 9 and 10 this is reduced, primarily by casting the answers in a similar form, and thereby demanding greater reliance on the content of both questions and answers as a basis for determining the sequence. However, many children will find it hard to grasp the point of sequencing exercises of the type used to test the skill.

Possibly the most useful remedial action that the teacher can take is in the direction of encouraging coherent communication and dialogue, and fostering continuity of expression in the child's written work. This aspect is, of course, likely to develop long before the child learns to read, if he is brought up in an atmosphere where extended communication is encouraged. It is by no means uncommon to find pre-school children brought up in articulate households with a grasp of sequencing which is entirely adequate to the demands of this test. Should the child be capable of speech of this order, then the most necessary thing is to encourage him to translate this skill into writing.

Unusually high scores
Such a score indicates a very satisfactory basis for future development. If the child has any unusually low scores, or one score which is rather below the two upon which the median is based, this should be considered, as it may suggest ways in which to develop his potential.

Subtest D: Comprehension

The rationale of the items
This section is concerned with the end-purpose of reading: understanding. It is intended to be a generalised test of overall reading competence.

Page 11: This block of items requires the child to select from the picture the appropriate piece of writing, and, to a minor extent, to draw appropriate conclusions. Thus, questions 1, 2, 5, 6 (Form A) and 2, 4, 6, 7 (Form B) ask the child only to extract information from the picture, whereas the remainder require some element of inference, and an answer in the appropriate mode demanded by the question.

Page 12: Although similar in form to page 11, this requires rather more reading, and the questions require the child to draw some conclusions from what he has read. Children can be helped to more constructive, intelligent reading if they are encouraged to elicit the meaning of what is given, by inference.

Pages 13–14: These pages require the child, given a very short and simple passage of prose, or near-prose, to take the imaginative step from what somebody says, to how they are feeling, and to summarise this in a different form of words. The structure of the passages is very simple, as is much of the vocabulary, but the imaginative leap involved in drawing conclusions about another's state of mind from what they say is still fairly new to the children, and some find it difficult. It might be argued that this is as much a spoken as a written skill, but it is, none the less, the proper province of the teacher of English.

Unusually low scores
An unusually low score on this test implies failure, as yet, to integrate the mechanics of reading, and put them to good use. Teachers should take great care that these skills do develop: no child will read happily unless he discerns a reason for doing so. However, to think in terms of immediate remedial action is probably wrong. Instead, one should endeavour, as all teachers normally do, to instil some awareness of the joy and discovery of reading, as a means to another world. Nevertheless, attention should always be given to the child with a low score on this subtest.

A great deal may be extracted from the child's responses to questions. The responses to this subtest are especially revealing of copying, or wandering attention – for example if one finds a mistake which links a few children, or a group of answers applicable to the other test form. A child with a clear grasp of his own limitations, and reasonable confidence, will write in the answers he knows, and omit those he doesn't. A child who does not have a clear understanding of the meaning of the questions may continue to answer 'yes' or 'no', even when this is not appropriate, or pick up random words from the questions, and repeat them. This is a very good guide to guessing in the earlier parts. In between there comes a child who can understand that, for example, question 3 on page 11 (Form A) refers to the shop, and therefore writes 'florist', or 'Mrs Tulip', rather than 'flowers'.

Unusually high scores
Such a score is, to some extent, the point of it all. The child is reading with understanding. Look at the scores which fall below the median for indications of where the child may, in future, be held back, if at all.

Development

The **Edinburgh Reading Test** series was first commissioned by the Scottish Education Department and the Educational Institute of Scotland to meet a growing demand from teachers for an instrument to help them assess their pupils' progress in reading. Four tests make up the series: **ERT 1**, **2** and **4** were constructed by the Godfrey Thomson Unit for Academic Assessment at the University of Edinburgh, and **ERT3** was produced by Moray House College of Education: both are now part of the Faculty of Education at the University of Edinburgh. The initial work was carried out under the guidance of a steering committee including representatives from all four bodies, with practising teachers from the Educational Institute of Scotland, and educational psychologists from both Edinburgh and Strathclyde Universities.

This third edition of **ERT1** has been revised and restandardised by the Educational Assessment Unit at the University of Edinburgh.

The standardisation sample

The tables for conversion of total raw scores to standardised scores, percentiles and reading ages are based on the performance of 8200 children tested in 2001. These children were drawn from 21 state primary schools in Scotland, 208 state primary schools in Somerset and 50 state primary schools in other parts of England. The Scottish schools were mainly located in South Fife and Aberdeenshire while those in England other than Somerset were mainly located in Lincolnshire and Berkshire. Data from the schools in England were chosen in such a way that the proportions of children who in 2000 achieved Level 4 or above in the English national tests administered at Key Stage 2 were matched to the national average. Further details can be obtained from the DfES website http://www.dfes.gov.uk/.

The ages of these children were distributed as shown:

	7:0–7:4	7:5–7:9	7:10–8:2	8:3–8:7	8:8–9:0
Scotland	132	200	171	80	66
England	157	2929	2784	1479	207

Means and standard deviations

The raw-score means and the raw-score standard deviations by sexes in the two areas were as follows:

		N	Mean	Standard Deviation
Scotland	*Boys*	362	63.63	22.03
	Girls	302	70.01	18.64
England	*Boys*	4036	65.99	21.65
	Girls	3876	72.13	18.14

Standardisation: total scores

The standardisation of the whole test is based on the scores of all 8200 children in the sample between the ages 7:0 and 9:0. The conversion table gives standardised scores based on a normal distribution with a mean of 100 and a standard deviation of 15. The allowance for age is sensitive to alterations between standardised score levels. It is calculated on the basis of thirteen linear regressions of score upon age at fixed percentiles. These percentiles correspond to standardised scores at five-point intervals from 70 to 130. Intermediate standardised scores were obtained by linear interpolation.

The subtests

The subtest means are given below by country and by gender. Overall the girls did better than the boys on all subtests, the differences between averaged means being, in descending order of magnitude, those for subtests Syntax, Sequences, Comprehension and Vocabulary.

Children from England did better than Scottish children in each of the subtests, the differences between averaged means being, in descending order of magnitude, those for subtests Syntax, Sequences, Vocabulary and Comprehension.

		Vocabulary	Syntax	Sequences	Comprehension
Scotland	*Boys*	16.16	20.63	13.54	13.30
	Girls	17.06	22.50	15.51	14.95
England	*Boys*	16.51	21.59	14.15	13.73
	Girls	17.52	23.70	15.72	15.19

Subtest means for five age-groups are as follows:

Age-group	Vocabulary	Syntax	Sequences	Comprehension
7:0–7:4	15.45	19.53	12.62	11.87
7:5–7:9	16.46	21.59	14.16	13.59
7:10–8:2	17.14	22.92	15.20	14.68
8:3–8:7	17.59	23.66	15.75	15.51
8:8–9:0	18.46	25.03	16.62	16.42

The next table gives the means for each subtest and for the test as a whole for Form A and Form B of the test. The two groups (of approximately 1450 pupils each) were not precisely matched, as the distribution of scripts to pupils was under the control of each school, but the profiles of scores should, if the forms are equivalent, be very similar. The table shows that this is the case.

	Vocabulary	Syntax	Sequences	Comprehension	Whole test
Form A					
Mean	16.96	22.24	14.93	14.19	68.32
Standard Deviation	3.88	6.79	5.11	5.40	19.61
Form B					
Mean	17.59	23.42	15.24	15.24	71.50
Standard Deviation	3.75	6.71	5.09	5.37	19.15

Subtest intercorrelations

Product-moment correlations between the subtests were calculated on the basis of the raw scores from the whole standardisation sample. Their values are given in the table below. The correlations are in general high, given the length and reliability of the subtests.

	Syntax	Sequences	Comprehension
Vocabulary	0.860	0.775	0.828
Syntax		0.811	0.846
Sequences			0.803

High and low subtest scores

The scores singled out on the subtests as of special interest are not to be equated with statistically significant scores. Table 4, on page 24, gives the range of subtest scores which may be expected for a pupil whose score on the test as a whole falls in a given band. These ranges were obtained as follows. For the pupils in the standardisation sample, the score on each subtest was regressed against the total score on all subtests to obtain the least squares line. The 95% confidence limits of this line were calculated – i.e. the two lines parallel to the least squares line and equidistant from it which exclude 5% of the standardisation sample. The two lines were then used to find the subtest scores corresponding to the score at the centre of each band.

Reliability and homogeneity

Reliability should really be called *replicability* or *stability*. It is the extent to which a pupil would get the same test score if he or she had done the test on a different day or had done a different form of the test, if one exists. It is measured by determining how far the score on one question can be predicted from the same pupil's scores on other questions in the test. This in turn depends on two things. The first is how many other questions there are (since the more questions there are, the better they will collectively be as a basis for prediction). The second is how closely the scores on the different questions correlate with each other (since the more they correlate with each other, the more accurately can they be used to predict each other). A reliability of one means that

exactly the same score would have been obtained on another occasion. A reliability of zero means we have no idea what the score would have been on another occasion. Reliability is calculated using the Kuder-Richardson formula 20 (KR20).

A concept related to reliability is that of *homogeneity*. If the various items in the test measure the same thing, then it should be expected that, over a group of pupils, items should show high levels of intercorrelation. On the other hand, if items are accessing different skills or attainments, then they should show lower levels of intercorrelation. A test where all the items measure the same thing is said to be homogeneous and it is possible to measure the degree of homogeneity which any test shows. If its value is zero, there is no intercorrelation between the items and the sum is meaningless. If its value is one (the maximum), then the items show the largest possible amount of intercorrelation, given the proportions of pupils getting each item correct. As noted above, homogeneity is one of the determinants of reliability: it can be thought of as reliability with the effect of test length taken out. Homogeneity is calculated using Loevinger's coefficient.

Kuder-Richardson reliabilities (KR20) and Loevinger homogeneity values were calculated on the basis of a sample of 561 scripts from across the standardisation sample. KR20, for the 91 items, was 0.97 while the whole test homogeneity was 0.39. Separate reliability and homogeneity values were also calculated for the four subtests. Their values, which are highly satisfactory for subtests of these lengths, are set out below.

	Vocabulary	Syntax	Sequences	Comprehension
Reliability	0.90	0.91	0.89	0.90
Homogeneity	0.47	0.36	0.38	0.48